MW01248021

Chakra
for
Beginners

5 BOOKS IN 1

The Complete Updated Guide To
Increase Energy Healing, Awaken And
Balance Chakras, Master The Most
Advanced Kundalini Awakening And
Reiki Healing Techniques

By

New Mindfulness Lab

TABLE OF CONTENTS

ENERGY HEALING:

INTRODUCTION 19
CHAPTER ONE: WHAT IS ENERGY HEALING 21
    HISTORY..22
    BELIEFS...22
    SCIENTIFIC INVESTIGATION..23
        DETACHED HEALING 23
        CONTACT HEALING 24
        EVIDENCE-BASE 24
        EXPLANATION FOR AFFIRMATIVE FEEDBACK 24
    CLASSIFICATION OF ENERGY HEALING....................................25
CHAPTER TWO: TYPES OF ENERGY HEALING 27
    SOUND HEALING THERAPY..27
        TYPES OF SOUND THERAPY 27
        HOW SOUND HEALING WORKS..30
        BENEFITS OF SOUND HEALING..30
        INSTRUMENTS USED IN SOUND HEALING 30
    TOUCH THERAPY...30
        REIKI.. 31
        THERAPEUTICAL TOUCH.. 35
    ETF 41
        ADVANTAGES OF ETF 42
    ACUPUNCTURE...42
        CLINICAL RESEARCH..44
        NEEDLES 45
        RELATED SEARCHES 47
        EFFICIENCY 49
        PUBLICATION BIAS 50
        SPECIFIC CONDITIONS... 51
        BENEFITS OF ACUPUNCTURE...54
        EXPECTATIONS IN SESSION... 55
        RISKS 55
        HOW TO FIND A PRACTITIONER 56
    CRYSTAL HEALING...56
        SCIENTIFIC EVIDENCE... 57
    QIGONG...58
        BENEFITS OF QIGONG...59
        SAFETY AND COST 59
    INTUITIVE HEALING...60
        HOW IT WORKS 60

BALANCE CHAKRAS:

INTRODUCTION **119**

CHAPTER 1 .... **121**

FUNDAMENTALS OF CHAKRA BALANCE............................... **121**

CHAPTER 2.. **123**

THE ROOT CHAKRA **123**

    SYMPTOMS OF AN UNHEALTHY ROOT CHAKRA 123
    ROOT CHAKRA BLOCKAGE.. 124
    HOW TO HEAL THE ROOT CHAKRA....................................... 125

CHAPTER 3... **128**

THE SACRAL CHAKRA **128**

    SYMPTOMS OF AN UNHEALTHY SACRAL CHAKRA...................... 128
    SACRAL CHAKRA BLOCKAGE... 129
    HEALING SACRAL CHAKRA 130

CHAPTER 4.. **133**

THE SOLAR PLEXUS **133**

    SYMPTOMS OF AN UNHEALTHY SOLAR PLEXUS......................... 133
    SOLAR PLEXUS BLOCKAGE.. 134
    HEALING THE SOLAR PLEXUS 134

CHAPTER 5.. **137**

THE HEART CHAKRA.. **137**

    SYMPTOMS OF AN UNHEALTHY HEART CHAKRA........................ 138
    HOW TO HEAL YOUR HEART CHAKRA 139

CHAPTER 6.. **143**

THE THROAT CHAKRA **143**

    SYMPTOMS OF AN UNHEALTHY THROAT CHAKRA...................... 144
    THROAT CHAKRA BLOCKAGE.. 145
    WHAT DOES A NOURISHED AND BALANCED THROAT CHAKRA
    LOOK LIKE? 145
    HEALING OF THE THROAT CHAKRA 145

CHAPTER 7 ....**151**

THIRD EYE CHAKRA..**151**

    SYMPTOMS OF AN UNHEALTHY THIRD EYE CHAKRA 152
    THIRD EYE CHAKRA BLOCKAGE.. 153
    HEALING THE THIRD EYE CHAKRA..................................... 154

CHAPTER 8... **161**

THE CROWN CHAKRA.. **161**

CHAKRA AWAKENING:

CHAKRAS 227

THEIR MEANING AND SIGNIFICANCE 227

WHAT ARE CHAKRAS? 227
THE FIRST CHAKRA - MULADHARA CHAKRA 229
THE SECOND CHAKRA - SVADHISHTHANA CHAKRA 231
THE THIRD CHAKRA - MANIPURA CHAKRA 232
THE FOURTH CHAKRA - ANAHATA CHAKRA 233
THE FIFTH CHAKRA - VISHUDDHA CHAKRA 235
THE SIXTH CHAKRA - AJNA CHAKRA 235
THE SEVENTH CHAKRA - SAHASRARA CHAKRA 236

CHAPTER 2 238

CHAKRA AWAKENING TUTORIAL 238

WHAT DOES IT MEAN TO AWAKEN THE CHAKRAS? 238
HOW TO AWAKEN THE CHAKRAS 238
EXERCISES 239
WHAT IS THE THIRD EYE? 258
HOW TO ACTIVATE THE THIRD EYE 263
TECHNIQUES FOR AWAKENING YOUR THIRD EYE 264
HOW TO ILLUMINATE THE POWER OF THE THIRD EYE CHAKRA266
HOW TO DEAL WITH THE DANGERS OF OPENING THE THIRD EYE
.... 267

CHAPTER 4 269

THE PINEAL GLAND 269

WHAT IS THE PINEAL GLAND AND WHAT ARE ITS FUNCTIONS?.269
HOW TO ACTIVATE THE PINEAL GLAND 270
WHY IS THE PINEAL GLAND BLOCKED? 270
ACTIVATE MELATONIN PRODUCTION 273
TIPS TO NATURALLY MAINTAIN A GOOD LEVEL OF MELATONIN 273
THE MIRACLES OF THE NETTLE 274
OTHER BASIC METHODS WITH WHICH YOU CAN START WORK ON
THE ACTIVATION OF THE PINEAL GLAND 275

CHAPTER 5 278

KUNDALINI AND THE POWER OF THE CHAKRAS 278

KUNDALINI INTRODUCTION AND OVERVIEW 278
WHY IS IT IMPORTANT TO LEARN AND PRACTICE KUNDALINI .. 280
AWAKENING AND ASCENSION OF KUNDALINI 281
MANTRA JAPA 282
THE BLESSING OF SAINTS AND TEACHERS 283
THE HEALTH BENEFITS OF KUNDALINI 291

CHAPTER 6 294

KUNDALINI - PRACTICAL TIPS AND NOTES 294

CLEARING OUT NEGATIVE ENERGY 295
BLOCKAGES THAT PREVENT KUNDALINI FROM RISING
SMOOTHLY, AND HOW TO CLEAR THESE BLOCKAGES 295

CHAPTER 7 300

CHAKRA MEDITATION:

INTRODUCTION TO REIKI 349
REIKI HEALING FOR ANXIETY & STRESS 351
ANXIETY...351
COMMON SYMPTOMS OF ANXIETY 351
CAUSES OF ANXIETY DISORDERS 353
STRESS..354
COMMON SYMPTOMS OF STRESS 354
CAUSES OF STRESS 355
HOW REIKI CAN HELP..356
SO WHY 21 DAYS OF REIKI?...357
CONNECTING WITH YOUR INTUITION AGAIN.....................361
INTUITION BUILDING EXERCISES 362
SET CHALLENGES FOR YOURSELF..365
GET OUT OF YOUR COMFORT ZONE.......................................365
WALK IN OTHER PEOPLE'S SHOES 366
ANALYZE YOUR THOUGHTS AND BELIEFS 367
KEEP A CURIOUS MIND...368
DEEPEN YOUR UNDERSTANDING 368
BECOME MORE AWARE OF THE DETAILS 369
FOCUS ON YOUR EMOTIONS 370
DEEPEN YOUR OBJECTIVENESS 371
LISTEN TO INNER GUIDANCE..371
PAY ATTENTION TO YOUR DREAMS...372
WRITE IT DOWN..373
PSYCHIC SKILL DEVELOPMENT 373
THE BASICS OF TELEKINESIS...373
EXERCISES TO DEVELOP YOUR TELEKINESIS 375
THE BASICS OF PYROKINESIS 377
EXERCISES TO DEVELOP YOUR PYROKINESIS 378
THE BASICS OF EMPATHY..380
BE GRATEFUL AND EXPRESS GRATEFULNESS WHENEVER
POSSIBLE 381
LOVE YOURSELF FULLY..382
AWARE AND MINDFUL BREATHING..382
EXERCISES TO DEVELOP YOUR EMPATHY 384
THE BASICS OF ASTRAL PROJECTION 384
EXERCISES TO DEVELOP YOUR ASTRAL TRAVEL SKILLS.........384
THE RISKS AND BENEFITS OF PSYCHIC SKILLS 386
CHAPTER 4 389
ROOT CHAKRA REIKI MEDITATION FOR DAY ONE THROUGH
THREE...389
OVERVIEW OF THE MOOLADHARA CHAKRA - ROOT OR 1ST
CHAKRA...389
RESPONSIBILITIES OF THE ROOT CHAKRA 390
IMBALANCE SYMPTOMS..390
DAY 1 ROOT CHAKRA PHYSICAL MEDITATION 391
DAY 2 ROOT CHAKRA MENTAL MEDITATION 393
DAY 3 ROOT CHAKRA SPIRITUAL MEDITATION 394
CHAPTER 5..396
SACRAL CHAKRA REIKI MEDITATION DAY FOUR THROUGH SIX396
OVERVIEW OF THE SVADHISTHANA CHAKRA - SACRAL OR 2ND
CHAKRA...396
RESPONSIBILITIES OF THE SACRAL CHAKRA............................397

IMBALANCE SYMPTOMS......397
DAY 4 SACRAL CHAKRA PHYSICAL MEDITATION......398
DAY 5 SACRAL CHAKRA MENTAL MEDITATION......399
DAY 6 SACRAL CHAKRA SPIRITUAL MEDITATION......400
CHAPTER 6......401
SOLAR PLEXUS CHAKRA REIKI MEDITATION DAY SEVEN THROUGH NINE......401
OVERVIEW OF THE MANIPURA CHAKRA - SOLAR PLEXUS OR 3RD CHAKRA......401
RESPONSIBILITIES OF THE SOLAR PLEXUS......402
IMBALANCE SYMPTOMS......402
DAY 7 SOLAR PLEXUS CHAKRA PHYSICAL MEDITATION......404
DAY 8 SOLAR PLEXUS CHAKRA MENTAL MEDITATION......404
DAY 9 SOLAR PLEXUS CHAKRA SPIRITUAL MEDITATION......405
CHAPTER 7......406
HEART CHAKRA REIKI MEDITATION DAY TEN THROUGH TWELVE......406
OVERVIEW OF THE ANAHATA CHAKRA - HEART OR 4TH CHAKRA......406
RESPONSIBILITIES OF THE HEART CHAKRA......407
IMBALANCE SYMPTOMS......407
DAY 10 HEART CHAKRA PHYSICAL MEDITATION......408
DAY 11 HEART CHAKRA MENTAL MEDITATION......409
DAY 12 HEART CHAKRA SPIRITUAL MEDITATION......409
CHAPTER 8......411
THROAT CHAKRA REIKI MEDITATION DAY THIRTEEN THROUGH FIFTEEN......411
OVERVIEW OF THE VISHUDDHA CHAKRA - THROAT OR 5TH CHAKRA......411
RESPONSIBILITIES OF THE THROAT CHAKRA......412
IMBALANCE SYMPTOMS......412
DAY 13 THROAT CHAKRA PHYSICAL MEDITATION......413
DAY 14 THROAT CHAKRA MENTAL MEDITATION......413
DAY 15 THROAT CHAKRA SPIRITUAL MEDITATION......414
CHAPTER 9......416
THE THIRD EYE REIKI MEDITATION DAY SIXTEEN THROUGH EIGHTEEN......416
OVERVIEW OF THE AJNA CHAKRA - THIRD EYE OR 6TH CHAKRA......416
RESPONSIBILITIES OF THE THIRD EYE CHAKRA......417
IMBALANCE SYMPTOMS......417
DAY 16 THIRD EYE CHAKRA PHYSICAL MEDITATION......419
DAY 17 THIRD EYE CHAKRA MENTAL MEDITATION......419
DAY 18 THIRD EYE CHAKRA SPIRITUAL MEDITATION......420
CHAPTER 10......421
CROWN CHAKRA REIKI MEDITATION DAY NINETEEN THROUGH TWENTY-ONE......421
OVERVIEW OF THE SAHASRARA CHAKRA - CROWN OR 7TH CHAKRA......421
RESPONSIBILITIES OF THE CROWN CHAKRA......422
IMBALANCE SYMPTOMS......422
DAY 19 CROWN CHAKRA PHYSICAL MEDITATION......423
DAY 20 CROWN CHAKRA MENTAL MEDITATION......424

REIKI HEALING:

DEEP WAVE 463
DEEP SOUND 464
DEEP GYMNASTICS... 464

CHAPTER 4 465

ENERGY HEALING INITIATION AND STEPS 465

INITIATION 467
STEPS 468
CIRCLE TRAINING 473
ORAL TRADITION 473
REIKI SYMBOLS 474

CHAPTER 5 477

LEARNING TO READ THE ENERGY FIELD 477

INCREASE POSITIVE ENERGY AND AVOID THE NEGATIVE ENERGY
.... 477
ENERGY MOVEMENT AND THE CHAKRA.................................478
UNLOCKING AND BALANCING THE CHAKRAS 478
WHEN ENERGY IS UNBALANCED OR BLOCKED? 479
IS THERE A UNIVERSAL PRACTICE FOR UNLOCKING
CHAKRAS?...480
FIRST CHAKRA 480
SECOND CHAKRA 481
THIRD CHAKRA.. 481
FOURTH CHAKRA... 482
FIFTH CHAKRA 482
SIXTH CHAKRA 483
SEVENTH CHAKRA..483

CHAPTER 6 485

THE CHAKRA MEDITATION - OPENING CHAKRAS IN MEDITATION
.... 485

EFFECTS OF CHAKRA MEDITATION 487

CHAPTER 7 489

ENERGY HEALING APPLICATION 489

HAND POSITIONS FOR ENERGY HEALING..............................489
THE MAIN POSITIONS FOR THE HEAD 489
THE MAIN POSITIONS FOR THE FRONT OF THE BODY 490
THE MAIN POSITIONS FOR THE BACK.................................. 491
ADDITIONAL POSITIONS... 491
EXPERIENCING PRESENCE - TREATMENT SESSION CONDITIONS
....492
REIKI EXERCISES...493
LEARN HOW TO BE MINDFUL DURING ENERGY HEALING 497

CHAPTER 8 498

PRACTICAL CLASSES FOR YOU!....................................... 498

GASSHO 498
REIJI HO..499